Simple Scripts to
Support Your People

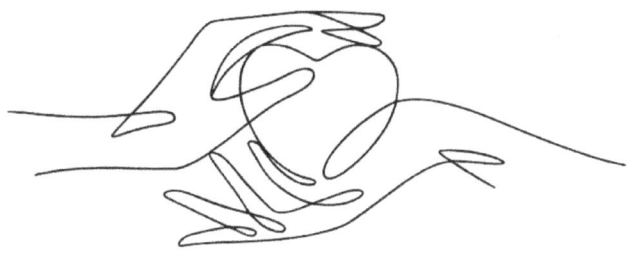

Genevieve "Jenny" Dreizen
Olivia Dreizen Howell

Long Island, New York

FIRST EDITION
This book was set in 10-17 pt. Times New Roman by
Fresh Starts Registry

v17042023

ISBN 979-8-9881059-4-7

Published by Fresh Starts Registry
Distributed by Fresh Starts Registry

FreshStartsRegistry.com

for our people.

foreword

As sisters, we have always had a pathological need to support others, and yes, it is probably something we should discuss with our therapist. But for the time being, we're sharing our incredible desire to support others, with you. We often find ourselves checking with the other sister to proof a text and make sure it is as loving, supportive and nourishing as we intend. We are just as often asked to review texts, emails and pre-phone-call notes from our people who just want to properly love their people. *Sometimes, you just don't know what to say, and we wanted to take the overwhelm out of those moments.*

These scripts should serve as a guide for tough, trying, and tremendous life moments. When writing these scripts and picking our scenarios we drew from our current experiences and crafted scripts to illustrate those life moments. When an experience arose that we did not personally live through, we human-checked the script with someone who has, because even the minute language details matter, and you matter.

This book is the first volume of the scripts you will need to support your people, and subsequent volumes will contain different specific situations and scripts. We want to hear your needs and what scripts you want to see in our next volume.

We're here to support you in supporting your people. We're proud of you. And we've got you.

Here's everything to say when you don't know what to say.

we made you something

the VASE Method

Knowing what to say and how to say it can be difficult, and there are so many specific scenarios we cannot account for when you are supporting your people. So we built you a method. It's called the VASE Method, and it stands for: Validate, Acknowledge, Support and Express. It's like bringing someone flowers: you want to make it easy for them to receive your words. And, just like with flowers, you'd present them in a vase.

We'll explain.

Validate: Recognize and honor that their experience is real and true. Demonstrate the truth and value of their lived experience.

Acknowledge: Ground them in their reality by illustrating the acceptance of their moment and feelings. Offer an understanding of their personal truth.

Support: Demonstrate your support by offering what you realistically can do to lighten their mental, physical, or emotional load.

Express: Tell them how you feel – and don't hold back! We give you full permission to love on your loved ones. Express your pride, love, respect, and compassion.

4

VASE Examples

Validate	Oh friend, I imagine this moment is so hard and scary.
Acknowledge	You may be having so many overwhelming feelings, and that's totally understandable.
Support	I'm just a text away if you need anything, day or night. I can do a quick Google search on any scary words. Do you need me to call your parents?
Express	I'm so sorry you're going through this, and I love you so much. You're not alone and we will get through this together.

VASE Examples

Validate	Well hello, friend! Thank you for sharing this exciting news!
Acknowledge	What a special time in your life, and I'm so proud of you. You should be so proud of yourself.
Support	I want to hear how everything went down – can we FaceTime later so you can give me all of the details?
Express	You are an amazing human and I'm so honored to celebrate you today and all days!

VASE Examples

Validate	Thank you for sharing that you're having a tough time. As exciting as life can be, it sure can be full of low moments too.
Acknowledge	I would imagine right now it feels really heavy to do simple tasks, but please know you're not alone.
Support	I'm here to pick up meds, or send you some TV show ideas, or sit with you on Zoom while you rest so you don't feel alone ever.
Express	I'm so proud of you for reaching out and I want you to know how incredibly loved you are.

how to use this book

We're so glad that you're here and that you picked up this book. Our scripts are a foundation. Build upon them: add, edit and embellish with details, names and specific tasks or support you can offer. You know your people best, allow our scripts to guide you and customize as needed.

Leaf through to find the script you need. We broke the scripts down into 5 major sections: Your People, Their Romantic Relationships, Their Community (Family and Friends), Their Kids, and Their Career. Within those major sections, the scripts are in no particular order - as we believe that every moment is important, every feeling is valid, and everyone you love deserves the support and celebration when they need it.

The fact that you've reached for this book in a time of need tells us that you are a loving, compassionate, and supportive human, and we have no doubt that those intentions will come through in all of your communications. Text these scripts, email them, leave them as a voicemail, or as the basis of a phone call or conversation in person. These scripts can be used over and over and across all platforms. We hope they help. We want to support you so that you can support your people.

ten ways to support someone

1. **Be in the moment with them.** Sometimes we just need to know that someone else is there with us in the moment. This is as simple as staying on video chat with them – no one even needs to talk. You're just there to support them so that they don't feel alone. Bonus points for video chatting with their kids so that they can do literally anything else (shower, call a doctor/lawyer/etc, drink a cup of coffee in silence).

2. **Check in with texts.** It sounds simple, but you'd be amazed how transformative a check-in, that requires nothing in response, and puts no emotional labor on the receiver, can be. People just want to be remembered and seen, and this is a really quick and easy way to make someone feel both.

3. **Check in on them.** Quietly check in to make sure they've eaten, drank some water and got just a bit of Vitamin D. Of course, in a non-forceful, loving way, such as a text or audio message. Don't hesitate to ask if they want you to send some meal suggestions or recipes as a bonus. Send them a text of a few simple meal ideas they can easily throw together (we're talking pasta, sauce, and cheese easy).

4. **Send appropriately distracting media.** For example, TV shows that won't make them think of their situation (like, don't send them a romance reality show during a breakup). Maybe some interesting podcasts that will occupy their mind with something new. Or, perhaps books that will make them laugh or send them down a rabbit hole of pop culture fun. And, don't forget about creating a playlist of important songs to help them feel distracted for a few minutes – the modern equivalent of the timeless tradition of a mixtape.

5. **Do the strategic research and logistical planning for them.** Often when someone is going through a big life change there are so many decisions to make and so much research to be done. It's just overwhelming. Support your person by looking into options for them, whether that's for new bedsheets, possible schools or even insurance plans. Help them make pros and cons lists, develop questions for meetings with a lawyer, map out their route from possible jobs to their new apartment, compile a list of doctors, or even help them write a script for handling stressful family situations. There are so many ways to support someone by easing the mental load of planning and life strategy.

6. **Just listen.** Listen to them cry and celebrate and vent and express. Receive their words with no judgment. Do not offer advice unless specifically requested.

7. **Make phone calls for them.** Sometimes calling a new person is too scary, but weirdly it's not as scary when it's for someone else. Make an appointment, reservation or call to lodge a complaint for your person. This can work for email too! Take just one thing off their plate if you can.

8. **Google the scary shit.** Sometimes it can be really scary to hear new terminology during a life change, for example: a legal phrase during a divorce, a medical word during a diagnosis, or even a contract term during the purchase of a house. Your job is to act as a gentle Google, filtering the new information to them in a way that they can safely access.

9. **Give them loving, conscious space if that's what they need**. Let them know you are there when they're ready, but recognize that sometimes we just need to know the support exists, but aren't ready to access it yet.

10. **Ground them.** Most importantly, remind them of all that they are capable of, and of all they've done, and of what they mean to you. Telling your people that you love them is always a simple, yet powerful, form of support.

scripts about them

what to say to your friend who…

you haven't heard from in a while

Hey there friend, was thinking about you and wanted to see how you are. Hope all is well and life is treating you as grand as you are. Would love to catch up soon, but no pressure. Just know there are people in this world (ME!) who think you're the absolute greatest. Love ya!

what to say to your friend who is...

buying a house

I'm so excited for you! And so proud of you. I can't wait to hear all about your plans. Send me the address so I can send a little treat, and look it up on Zillow, obviously. Congrats!

what to say to your friend who is...

deserving of celebration

Cheers to you, my darling friend! You are marvelous and deserving of wonderful things, delicious food, great music and lovely companions. I celebrate you everyday, but today especially. Know that you are so loved and lauded, always! Sending you hugs and a high five!

experiencing a depressive episode

My sweet friend, I am so sorry you're in a rough place right now. I am here for you whether you have the ability to reach out or not. I can come over and tidy up while you shower. I'll throw your towels in the dryer so you have nice warm towels to comfort you after. Or I can check in once a day with GIFs of kittens yawning. I love you and want to remind you this won't last forever, but I will be here for it all. You are so loved, and I'm here. You are not alone.

being shamed for being childfree

First of all: who the hell are these people? On your behalf, they are not allowed to talk to you like that. Listen, love, people have a lot of ideas of what they think is right, usually they need to believe the path they walked is the right and only one to go down. The good news is that's simply not true. And the better news is their judgements are their own problem and none of your business. I am so sorry they confronted you with their ridiculous ideas. Your choices are your own, and I am proud of you for knowing what you want and how you want your life to look. I'm here to vent it out with you, if you'd like. I'm also here to tell you how dope your choices and life are, and how proud of you I am. Like always, let me know if you need to hear how freaking fantastic you are, and I'll show up with a verbal cheerleading section. You're killing it at life.

21

feeling a lot of envy

Dude, I get it. Envy and jealousy are not our most attractive emotions, but they happen, and that's okay. Be kind to yourself and let it wash over you. No feeling lasts forever. What about their situation is something that you want? Let's identify that bit and then try to see how you can attain it in a way that makes sense in your life. I'm here for all of your feelings, the beautiful ones and the less than attractive ones. I love you, see you, and support you in all of your feelings.

what to say to your friend who...

found a lump in their breast

I know that you're scared and thinking of all of the worst-case scenarios right now. Recognize the best-case scenarios, too. Remember that early detection is key, so you're already one step ahead. Whatever the outcome, we will face it together and take it one step at a time. I'm always here to lend a shoulder to cry on, to nudge you to drink your water, to hug you, and to remind you to get off Google. I love you lots, and you're not alone in this worry.

what to say to your friend who is...

stepping into their truth

My sweet friend, I am so proud of you for being brave and stepping into your truth. You are an inspiration to me and I am lucky to have you as my friend and to be a witness to your beautiful life. Your authenticity is one of your greatest strengths and I am here for you always. I have always adored you and I'm thrilled to get to know you more as you share yourself with me and the world. Let me know how I can support you right now. I'm happy to just be a sounding board or phone tree information if you'd like me to. I am always, always here for YOU, to support and celebrate!

having a big sad day

It's just one of those days, huh? I'm here! You can talk to me or we can just sit on the phone and do our own things. Sad days happen (sad weeks and months and years too!) and we just have to wade through them as best we can. I can handle your sad, so feel free to lean on me. I'll check in with you in a little bit and in the meantime, I'll send some Office GIFs.

graduating with a
hard earned degree

YAS! You did it! I am so proud of you! I know how hard you worked and how much effort, sacrifice and brain power you committed to this. You should be so proud of yourself. Let's celebrate with a treat soon! Please send me your registry link so I can get you something special because you deserve it! And now, enjoy the moment and take a little time to just bask in the glow of your big accomplishment! Woohoo!

having financial stress

Oh man, this stuff is tough. I am here to chat it through with you and can strategize about next steps. I'm here to help make lists, do research, or Google anything you need. I am holding so much space for the stress this causes and the anxiety that comes along with it. You are strong and smart and wonderful and I am so sure you will figure this out. You are not alone, I'm just a text away.

what to say to your friend who...

needs a little emotional caretaking

Hello sweet friend, thank you for reaching out. Feeling vulnerable and needing to be taken care of in any way can feel so scary. Good news is, I love you and I feel so fortunate to be the one you're coming to in this moment! Letting your people love and take care of you is a kindness. Let's chat/meet for a coffee so we can talk it through and figure out what you need, and most importantly so I can love on you! You are such a phenomenal friend and I'm excited at the opportunity to get to take care of you the way you take care of me.

being tortured by insurance

I understand how stressful dealing with insurance issues can be, especially when it comes to medical bills. I just want to validate that this stuff feels so scary, so important and so real and it is, but it is not insurmountable. Remember that you are not alone, and I am here for you. Let's work together to find solutions and resources to help you navigate this. I'm happy to call and talk to people on your behalf if you're overwhelmed. Or just act as a sounding board, or a venting board. You deserve access to the care you need, without financial stress. I love you and I'm here for you.

nervous about reaching

out to a therapist

First of all, I want you to take a deep breath and remember that you are strong, brave, and wonderful. Reaching out to a therapist is a huge deal, and I'm so proud of you for putting your mental health first. If you need me to make any calls or do any research, I'm your person! We'll find someone who works well with you, I promise. I am celebrating you for making this brave step in your mental health journey because you are so loved and deserve to feel your best inside and out.

just received a scary
medical diagnosis

Hey love, thank you for sharing that with me. I want to validate that this is a really tough moment, so please give yourself grace for any of the big feelings you're having right now. Getting medical news like this can be a mental-mindfuck, so please just be gentle with yourself right now. Have you eaten anything? Had some water? All you need to do is keep breathing, and we will all be here to support you along the way. Let me know if you want me to take notes, or head to Google, or send you funny memes. I'm just a text away and you are not alone. I love you so much.

what to say to your friend who...

missed their flight

UGHHHHH, that's a nightmare! How frustrating and annoying. Are they being helpful? Want me to send new flight options? Your trip will happen. This happens all the time. I am so sorry it's kicking off this way. Let me know if there's anything I can do to help!

starting chemo

Well, here we go. I'm glad we're at the point of beginning your healing process, even as tough and overwhelming as it may be. Do you have what you need? Can I send ice pops? I'm going to send you soft socks and a warm blanket for treatments. I am so sorry you have to go through this, but I'm so glad you are getting the treatment you need. You are always on my mind and supporting you is a priority, so please do not hesitate to reach out. I love you so much, and I am so proud of you.

trying to make new friends

You are such a cool badass and ANYONE will be so excited to call you a friend. Hello, I know this from living it! Trying to make friends as an adult is Olympic level brave and I am in awe of your willingness! You are so amazing and I am excited to meet your new friends one day.

dealing with addiction issues

First of all, I'm so proud of you for reaching out and talking to me. You know that I am in awe of your strength and love you dearly. Secondly, healing and recovery aren't linear, and you're doing the very best you can, I am endlessly proud of you for that. Remember that you are not defined by your addiction. You are an amazing, loving, passionate, wonderful human who is having a tough moment, but it won't always be hard. We all love you and we are here to support you in anything you need. You can always reach out to me, there is no shame in asking for support. You are worthy of everything beautiful in this world, and all of the support you need.

being attacked on the internet

Ugh, this just sucks. Why are people the worst? I'm so sorry you're going through this. It will pass, I promise. Close all of your tabs, delete the apps from your phone, and close your laptop. It's the perfect time to disconnect for a while. Do you want some movie or book recs? Remember, people on the internet don't actually know you, they don't know the amazing, wonderful person you are. Don't read the comments, and let me know if you need me to do anything. This will fizzle!

being forced to sell their home/move

What a time, what a moment. Things may seem really overwhelming and big right now, but you aren't alone. Can I help you research a realtor or look for apartment listings? Do you need me to FaceTime with the kids so you can talk to a lawyer without little ears listening? I'm right here if you need any support as you figure these next moves out. Remember, a house is just four walls, but a home is the energy inside of it and you have the best, most loving, and wonderful energy. I am so proud of you for adulting big-time right now, and I'm here to help.

being kicked out of their place

Ugh, this is a shitty situation and I'm so sorry you're having to deal with this. What can I do to help? I can come over to help you pack, I can FaceTime you while you pack. I can research new places and call realtors. I'm so proud of your bravery and adulting right now as you navigate this odd time. You aren't alone, I'm right here if you need to bounce ideas or vent. It may feel really overwhelming and hard right now, but I promise it won't always. I love you lots, buddy.

what to say to your friend who is...

being shamed for being happy solo

Oh sheesh, people! I'm so sorry people are saying crap things to you. People just looooove to project their shit onto anyone who seems to be living a happy and fulfilled life, especially if they are happy and single! You are kickass and I'm so proud of the beautiful life you have created for yourself. You are a gorgeous human and you are worthy of all of the happiness and joy in life. Ignore the haters, focus on all of the beautiful details in your life. You are completely amazing and anyone would be lucky to be in your orbit, babe.

experiencing burnout but won't rest

Hey you, I'm saying this because I adore and admire you, but you've got to rest or you just won't feel better. You are not doing yourself any favors by pushing yourself through this and you don't need to prove yourself to anyone. Let me love on you a bit! Can I bring over dinner, or can I send Doordash cash so you can order something cozy and delicious? Send me a picture of what you order so I know you're actually relaxing. Go take a hot shower and crawl into bed. I know there's so much to do, but nothing will get done if you keep moving at this pace. I love you and want you to prioritize yourself!

deciding to go to the authorities
after a sexual assault

I am here for you, and I support you. Remember that you are not alone and you have the right to speak out and seek justice. I can go with you, or call you right before and after. I am proud of you for heading down this road. Even though I wish you didn't have to be, you are so brave. You are not facing this alone, I've got you. I believe you, and I will always believe you.

has discovered new allergies

Allergies are so frustrating. I am so sorry you're discovering more things you can't eat/things you are allergic to. I am super good at Googling and would be happy to do some research for you to remove some of the overwhelm of this new found information. Text me what they said, and in the future I can make sure there is always something you can eat when we go out. It's so frustrating, but I know you always do the best job of taking care of yourself and I am here to support you however I can.

what to say to your friend who is...

experiencing bullying

I'm so sorry to hear this and that you're going through this. Thank you for trusting me with this information, I hate that this is something you're experiencing. No one should be treated like that. I am always going to be a safe place for you to share. How can we alleviate this situation? We can write a letter or script together so you feel prepared when you go to the powers that be or confront this person. I am such a big fan of yours and want to make sure your light keeps shining.

what to say to your friend who is…

experiencing gender dysphoria

Thank you for sharing how you feel with me. I imagine it feels very difficult, confusing and disconnected to feel dysphoria in your own body. I am here to listen to your experience and support you in any way I can. I can help find and call professionals who might be able to support your journey more holistically. You deserve to feel at home in your body. I love you and want you to feel ease in every way.

found out they have an STD

First of all, this is NOT your fault. I am here to figure this out with you. Let's see what the doctor says and what they recommend we do to support your body right now. Let me know what I can do to ease the worry right now. I can grab your prescription or go to the doctor with you, if you want. Call me after the doctor and we can come up with a plan. You are not alone!

getting a breast reduction

I am SO proud of you for choosing what feels right for your body! I am here for all the pre-surgery plans and anxiety. Let me know how I can help. You want me to send you cute smaller bras? You are a gorgeous human no matter what, and I'm just so glad you know what you need to feel your very best.

undergoing gender
reassignment surgery

My sweet friend, what a special decision you've made. I am so proud of you for making a choice that will bring you closer to feeling like your truest self. You deserve to feel at home in your body. Surgery of any kind is overwhelming and scary, adding to this, the significance of this surgery, and I see what a big and maybe emotional circumstance this is! Please let me know how I can best support you pre and post surgery. I am always, always here for you and want to show up in the way you need me most right now! So proud of you, so happy for you and love you so much!

getting tested for STDs

I'm so proud of you for being brave and getting these tests done. It's totally scary and I know that ignoring it feels less scary, but in the long run knowing what's going on with your body is way less scary, and super duper responsible. I can call you right before and after or meet you for coffee after your appointment. Remember, whatever the results are we will figure it out. Love you lots and I'm proud of you for prioritizing your health and body.

what to say to your friend who is...

having a terrible

roommate experience

Feeling stress in your own home is such a gross feeling, you deserve to feel safe and calm in your own home. I am here to vent to and also help you make a plan. Do you want me to send you links to noise canceling headphones? I am going to Venmo you so you don't have to make dinner tonight and can hide in your room while we figure this out. Let me know if you're ready for me to send you new room or apartment listings. We'll get through this crap time, I promise!

healing after a sexual assault

Sweet friend, you may feel really weird right now, and maybe totally disconnected from your body and life. You went through something very scary and you are so brave, I just wish you didn't have to be. What do you need right now? Do you need me to come wash your clothes and sheets? Can I FaceTime you and watch a movie together? This is a shitty time, and if you're feeling lonely and anxious, I am RIGHT HERE. Truly, always in your pocket. I love you so much, my beautiful friend. Life won't always feel this way, I promise. And, in the meantime, I'll make you a playlist and Venmo you for a hot cocoa. Holding you close.

seems to be joining a
sketchy community

I'm glad you've found some people you like and are making a home in this new community. As you were so excited, and I wanted to know more info to share in your excitement, I read some more about them, and there are some things I find a bit concerning. I'd love to discuss what I read with you. I want you to be safe, happy and surrounded by people with only the best of intentions. Can we walk through this information together and have an honest conversation about this community? I love you so much and only, only want the best for you.

just had their vacation canceled

Oh man, that totally sucks, and I am so sorry. What a huge bummer, I know you were looking forward to this trip, and this is so crappy! How can I help you pivot a little? What can we do? I recommend ordering food and wallowing for a little. Call me and I will rapid fire suggest a list of foods you can order. Do you need help reaching out to the airline/hotel/etc? The disappointment is so real, I am here to validate that for you!

had their luggage lost

Oh no! I am so sorry, what a terribly out of control feeling. Being without your things is so unnerving. Let's triage this, I am going to find local pharmacies to get your medications at. Maybe call your doctor for an emergency prescription? Send me the address of where you're staying so I can find some places for you to grab clothes and essentials. Your luggage WILL show up and we WILL make sure you get whatever is coming to you from the airline, but in the meantime let's make sure you have what you need.

moving

You are brave for taking this step and starting a new chapter in your life, and I am so proud of you! I will miss you being so close, but please know that I'm always in your pocket and just a text or FaceTime away. I can't wait to see the amazing things you do in your new home. Remember that I'm always here for you and I believe in you and all of your beautiful dreams!

nervous about going to the doctor

Blah, I know that going to the doctor can be a daunting task, my friend. But, I am so proud of you for putting yourself and your health first. Remember, you're not alone, and I'm legit always here for you. You have to take care of your health and well-being because you are so loved, and going to the doctor is a step in the right direction. You got this, babe!

no longer feeling connected to their wardrobe

I HATE that feeling of a full closet and nothing to wear. You want to chat a little about what's going on? Maybe if we talk we can try to figure out where your personal style wants to fall. Then maybe we can find some new or used items that fit the bill and we can do a little virtual fashion show. I am happy to send you style inspo pics or go shopping with you and be your hype person! You are magnificent and deserve to feel comfortable and confident in your clothes, so let's figure out how to get there.

what to say to your friend who is...

overwhelmed by packing

I know how overwhelming packing can be, but remember to take a deep breath and try to focus on one task at a time. Do you want me to FaceTime you and keep you company as you pack? I'm here to help, let me know if there's anything I can do to make it easier for you. Remember to get yourself a treat when you're done!

experiencing a relapse

Thank you for filling me in on what's going on. I am here for you and I love you, no matter what. From what I understand, relapsing can be difficult and can bring up a lot of feelings of sadness and depression. Remember that it's not a failure and it's a part of the recovery process. You are not alone, let's work together and get you the support you need to get back on track.

revealing abuse to you

I am so glad you came to me with this, and I am so sorry you have to live through this. I promise you, your story is safe with me, and we can move forward however you're comfortable, at your pace. You are so strong. Never forget that. What do you want to happen next? Remember, I am solidly, always here for you and love you so much.

revealing and/or healing from childhood sexual abuse

Oh, my darling friend, thank you for sharing that with me. I am so sorry that is something you survived. You did not deserve that, no one does. You deserved and deserve so much more, so much better. I am so glad that you feel safe telling me this. Do you feel like you need outside support? Can I help you find a therapist? I am constantly amazed at the person you are, and this adds another layer, you are so tough, but I am sorry you had to be. I am holding you in my heart.

spending their savings on something big and anxious about it

Ack, I totally understand that spending your savings on something big can be overwhelming, my friend. It can bring up a lot of feelings all over the place! Remember, you are not alone, I'm here for you, to listen and support you. It's important to remember that investing in yourself and your goals is an important step towards your happiness and well-being. Lean on me, and know that you are loved and respected.

stepping into their truth and afraid of response

I am so, so proud of you for living your truth. I love you so much, just exactly for who you are. I know it can be scary to share this news with others, but know that people's reactions are just that: theirs, and you cannot control them either way. Sometimes people need time to integrate information, sometimes people just can't handle reality. Either way I want to celebrate you, and your truth, and your bravery. I love you so much and am here to support you however I can.

what to say to your friend who is...

embracing their gender euphoria

My wonderful friend! I am so glad you are feeling at home in your own body! What a remarkable and wonderful sensation. You deserve this for so many reasons. I am always here to hear about your successes and joy and wins, so please lay it on me! So proud of you for pursuing your own joy.

trying to find a new hobby

First of all, kudos to you for trying to find something you like to do. What an existential experiment! I'd love to hear what you're brainstorming and about your new hobby once you've figured it out. Give me all the details! Proud of you for exploring your inner self.

weird about their birthday, but it's their birthday

Hello friend! You've told me in the past that today is a bit weird and complicated for you, so I am just going to drop this and run away – you don't have to respond! I am SO glad you exist, and so proud to know the person that you are. You are an amazing person to have in my life and I consider myself lucky to call you a friend! Check your email later for a coffee gift card, you deserve it!

what to say to your friend who…

you just miss

Friend! You're on my mind and I miss you! You are such an important person to me and your presence in my life brings me joy and light. I hope you always know and carry with you how loved you are!

what to say to your friend who…

you want to celebrate

I just wanted to remind you how absolutely AMAZING you are. I was thinking of you today and what a magical human you are! How lucky am I to have YOU in my life? I hope you're having the day you deserve!

you want to remind how much you love them

Hello my sweet friend, I just wanted you to know that I am thinking of you, and I think you're just totally the best. I hope you're having such a beautiful day, and hope that you eat something totally delicious, and that the road rises to meet you!

what to say to your friend who is...

alone on Valentine's Day

I know it's a silly day, but I just wanted you to know you are loved. 🩶

what to say to your friend who is…

in need of dance party

I think you need to get up, dance and move that body! I'm sending a playlist over right now, and demand that you get grooving. I'll be over here dancing, so we'll be dance-partying together. You are full of happiness and good vibes so let's dance to that!

scripts about relationships

what to say to your friend who is…

restocking their home after
a break up/move

It's so much right now, and I can imagine your brain is constantly pinging with things you need to get and do. How can I help? Do you want me to make a list of essentials? Can I help you build your registry so we can send it out to everyone? You deserve the support, and everyone who loves you wants to help and be there for you. I bet it seems like a lot, but let's have fun with this too. What are your favorite colors? Do you like little forks or big forks? You've made some really brave decisions, and now we get to restock your life with the items that bring you pure joy. I've got you, you're not alone. Let's do this together.

just got engaged

I am so happy for you and [their partner]! I wish I could be there to celebrate with you in person, but know that I am sending all my love and congratulations from afar. I can't wait to hear all the details and to see the ring!

got stood up for a date

WHAT! That is so ridiculous. Honestly, better to know now than later, right? You're probably all dressed up and looking so beautiful! I'm going to FaceTime you so that your LEWK does not go unappreciated!! This was clearly not your person, but I hate when people are so rude! No second chances for this one. I'm so sorry this happened, you're a gorgeous badass and people are the worst!

announcing their divorce

Congratulations on making such a brave decision. I know it wasn't easy, but you are worthy of every wonderful thing in this world. Divorce is a gift, and you are going to come out of this stronger and more powerful than ever before. I love you so much and I'm so damn proud of you. I'll check in soon to see how you're doing and know I'm always just a text away!

has a partner who doesn't listen

You deserve someone who listens to you and hears what you need. I support you in any decision you make, but you shouldn't have to get angry and cry to be heard. I love you and want you to be in a relationship with someone who values and respects your energy. I'm always here to listen.

what to say to your friend who is...

experiencing emotional abuse

First of all, thank you so much for sharing this with me. I'm so proud of you for being brave and speaking up, and please know, anything you say to me is confidential and safe. Your safety is my priority. You do not deserve to be treated like anything other than the amazing, brilliant and lovely person that you are. I am so sorry someone thought it was okay to treat you this way. It is not acceptable. How can I best support you right now? Be honest. What's the safest way to send you some therapists over? I'm happy to call them for you too. Thank you for trusting me with this. Please, please know that you don't deserve anything less than being treated like gold. I love you and we will walk through this together.

abandoning themselves
for a partner

I want you to know that I am so happy you found someone who you feel so strongly about and have so much love for. As someone who adores you, I just wanted to check in with you and make sure that you're still connecting with yourself and the amazing human I've always known. I know how it can be tricky to practice our hobbies / take time for self care things for ourselves when we're so happily wrapped up in the warmth of love, but I wanted to remind you how freaking kickass and rad you are, and make sure that your gorgeous wild heart is still getting its moment to shine. I'm proud of you, friend.

going through a mutual but

toxic break up

I can imagine it's so hard to split from someone that you had so much love and passion for, and I'm proud of both of you for making this brave decision together. I would love for you to share with me how you're feeling so I can make sure to support you as best I can. I also know sometimes when you split from your partner, you have all these stories to tell and texts to send, and you don't know where to send them, send them to me! Your stories always make me laugh and I love a good meme. I am here for you, for it all.

taking care of their partner

First of all, I think you are doing a beautiful job figuring out some very heavy shit. The balance of romance and life and caretaking is probably an impossible one to strike moment to moment and you are holding it all so well. I wish for both of you that you didn't have to be carrying all of this. I'm here for all of the worried and confused and overwhelmed texts, and more than ready to talk things through if a sounding board would help. Would it help to talk through your plan of how you're managing everything and if there's anything you can delegate to friends or family? I've got you both on my mind and want to be there to support you however I can.

was cheated on

Well, that fucking sucks. I am so sorry. How completely cruel and spineless. Cheating says everything about the cheater and nothing about the one who is cheated on. I would imagine you feel really crappy right now, and I just want you to know that you're a truly amazing human being and I'm so honored to be in your orbit. FaceTime me when you can so we can sing angry songs together. This is a huge betrayal and I want to validate that, as well as all of your other feelings. There are a lot of big feelings right now, but they won't last forever, and I will help you find your way out. I love you and you deserve so much better.

dealing with a coercive partner

My love, you deserve to feel safe in your home, physically, emotionally, psychologically, and spiritually. I am so sorry this is happening, and I'm so grateful you shared it with me. Let's talk about what we can do to start helping the situation. I'm here to Google to find you a therapist, lawyer, or a new place, whatever you need. Your safety and happiness are my priority. You are my priority. I love you and you are wonderful. Thank you for trusting me, I will be by your side as you figure this out.

dealing with coercive sexual control from a partner

People who love us care about how they make us feel. This isn't love. You are so wonderful and deserve to feel safe and loved and cared for. I know this is really scary and I never want to put you in more danger so let's figure out a safe way to handle this together. What can I do right now to make your tomorrow a little better and safer? I love you so much and I am so glad you felt safe enough with me to reveal this. You deserve so much better.

just discovered their ex's new partner on social media

Oh my! How NOT FUN is that!? Do you want me to go check this out? Maybe we should block them both so that you're not tempted to peek? I see how hard you're working to heal. Ugh, I'm so sorry. How are you feeling? What is this bringing up? Want to vent? Cry? I'm here to listen, and also to provide catty commentary. I'm really good at that! Love you, babe!

eloped

What! You two mad cats! Congratulations. I can't WAIT to see the pictures. I'd like to hear any and all details you want to share! How was the day? I'm so proud of you for choosing the path that brought you both joy and ease. You deserve so much love and happiness and I am so glad you found your person!

what to say to your friend who...

ended their engagement

My brave and wonderful friend! I know this wasn't an easy decision to make, but I am SO proud of you for choosing yourself and your joy. We can figure out all the cancellation stuff together, and I'm happy to phone tree this information to wedding guests or vendors. You deserve all the happiness in the world and I am sure this is a step in that direction. You may have some sad days ahead, but I will be here to check in on you and hold you in this time.

what to say to your friend who is…

ending a relationship because of distance

Ugh, I am so sorry, friend. This just sucks. I know how much you care about them, and also how difficult everything was. You can hold all of the emotions at once. Let me know if you need an ear to vent or cry to! I'm going to text you Tina Fey GIFs and check in with you. If you feel the need to text them, text me instead! It just sucks, I am so sorry. I'm here for anything. Love you lots.

ending a relationships because of differing values/belief

My friend, this is so hard, and I am sure that you're hurting. I'm so sorry, I wish there was an easy way through this time, but I just want you to know that you're not alone. Ever. I'm here if you need to cry on the phone, or need a movie recommendation (nothing about love!), or if you feel the need to text them, you can text me instead. The shitty truth is that sometimes love isn't enough, but YOU are enough, and I love you so much. I'm so proud of you for recognizing your needs and values, because you matter, and they matter, and never forget that.

experiencing emotional abuse around body

My beautiful friend, thank you for sharing this with me. I'm so sorry you're experiencing it. No one is allowed to make you feel less than amazing about your gorgeousness, it is totally unacceptable. Let me know how I can support you right now. Do you need to talk it out with someone? Do you need constant validation about how fantastic you are? Because I can do anything you need, I'm here for you. You are not alone. You are a fucking badass, sexy, beautiful human and I am proud to call you my friend. I love you lots and we got this.

feeling disconnected from
their partner

Feeling a disconnect is so rough, I'm so sorry you're experiencing that, it just feels terrible. It's a very confusing feeling to be in an uncomfortable place with the person you love, but I know you two can weather this and figure this out. You guys are strong and have been through a lot. Don't forget that connection and disconnection are cyclical. My advice would be to start simple and slow. Just try and enjoy a show or movie together, something low stakes to help get the connection ball rolling. It won't last forever. Text me if you want to brainstorm ideas. We got this.

formulating a plan to leave

Alright, let's do this. I am so damn proud of you. Do you want me to contact rentals for you? Attorneys? I realize it might be tough or dangerous for you to contact these people from home in case they hear/find out, so I can make any calls or do any research you need. I can come over to help pack/hang out on FaceTime while you pack. Oh, also I will send you a checklist for packing, would that help? I am in awe of your strength and bravery, and I hope you know how much you're loved! You are not alone in this for one second, we got you. It's going to be okay, I promise.

getting lost in wedding planning

Planning a wedding is such a range of emotions! How can I help? It's SO much to think about. Do you want to just walk through some of the plans and see what you can delegate to [your partner]? And, I'm here to do any research or make phone calls! I know it seems like a lot, and it *is* a lot, but you are not alone. You are doing a great job and it's going to be a beautiful, romantic and fun wedding. I'm so excited to be by your side for the journey and dance it out on the big day!

going no contact with

an ex-partner

Going no contact is a huge step and it seems really scary and overwhelming, but I am incredibly proud of you for putting yourself first. You, your mental health, and your future are all worth it. Remember, you are not alone, I'm here for you, to listen and support you through this process. You deserve to have a peaceful and healthy life, and I will be here to help you in any way that I can. Lean on me and know that you are loved.

got married and you couldn't be there

Today is the day! Somebody's getting marrrrried! I am so sorry I can't be there, but I love you and I know the day will be filled with absolute fun and joy. I legit cannot wait to see all the photos! Once you've had a good sleep and basked in the glow of the day and honeymoon, I cannot wait to hear every detail you remember. Sending my love to both of you today and always!

in the process of breaking up
with their partner

Breakups are never easy and are almost always a mess. You are doing a great job of walking through the process and grief, and I'm proud of you for taking steps in the direction of your joy. I'm here whenever you need me. Can you take a walk to get some space and time and air out your energy a bit? Why don't you call me while you walk and we can talk through the next steps? I am sure that the pain is intense and heavy, but it won't last, I promise. I love you and am so proud of you.

just found out that their ex *is* dating that person they suspected

First of all, you lovely genius, you knew! Good intuition! I am here to validate that, you totally, totally knew. I am sorry though, what a gross icky feeling. Do you want me to watch their IG stories for you so that you don't have to? Let's get a treat and you can vent if you want, and we can both marvel at your genius.

just had a big fight with their partner

Oh man, I'm so sorry, that feels so crappy. Fights are never fun. I'm here to listen, if you want to share. It's just the most fragile feeling. You guys will be fine, but I know how scary and big it can feel in the moment. Take a breath, turn on your favorite song, and go for a walk. I'm here if you need me.

just had their partner pass away

Oh my dear sweet friend. I am holding you in my heart and will hold you in my arms soon. It's so clear how much you loved [Beloved's Name]. I am so sorry that this is now part of your story. I am on my way and I will stroke your hair, warm your towels and change your sheets. You are never alone. Your community and I have you, we love you. We love [Beloved] so much, and mourn the loss alongside you. I'm here to call people, share information and make plans as much as you need. I'm going to keep texting you to make sure you're hydrated. You don't have to respond. I love you, friend.

was just served divorce papers

First of all, take a breath, sit down, and just breathe. Everything is probably overwhelming and scary right now but you are not alone. Do you want to text some photos of the papers over and I can read them too? I can do some Googling of scary terms and lingo. We're going to get through this and find your hype team who can help support you through this process. I know you're flipping out, but it's going to be okay, I promise. We will find a way through this together.

missing their significant other

Oh love, it is so hard to be away from the person who is your home. Soon enough you'll be in their arms again and all will feel right. In the meantime I can offer you Muppet GIFs, and you can text me all the sad/happy/sappy things you want about them. I can't imagine how you're feeling, and how tough it is to be away from them. I'm holding space for you. Honestly, I am so glad you found someone who you are so devastated to be away from! What a beautiful and heartbreaking thing!

what to say to your friend who is...

moving out of the home they shared with their now ex

What a moment! Let's get you packed and organized. I can come over/FaceTime you while you pack. They're not giving you any trouble right? If they are, let's figure out a plan to make sure you feel safe and protected while you're packing and moving. I am sending you a playlist to jam out to while you pack and a little Venmo to buy a moving day sandwich. I am going to text you to check in on progress and make sure you're drinking some water. You've got this. I am proud of you, this isn't easy but we're going to power through and it will be over before you know it.

what to say to your friend who...

requires care taking by
their partner

Oh love, it probably feels so vulnerable to need your partner to take care of you. It's hard to give up control, especially when it comes to our body. Remember that [partner] loves you and wants to help you through this! We all need help at different times and it's important you let [partner] show up for you and love on you when you need it. Let's navigate this together and find the support you need. You are wonderful and we are all here for you.

has new relationship anxiety

UGH, I know, it's so hard. The beginning is so exciting and also so anxiety ridden. Just know that you are so amazing and wonderful and whatever happens you WILL be okay. What's meant for us won't pass us by! Allow your anxiety to be felt, but don't trust in it, trust in your intuition and gut. And remember anyone who gets to spend time with you is VERY LUCKY. You are such a wonderful human and I couldn't love you more, anyone deserving will see that!

what to say to your friend who is…

planning a funeral for
their partner

My love, I am so sorry that this is something you are having to live through. Know that I see how hard you're working to hold it all together and I am holding space for you. Please, please, let me know how I can help right now. I can call people, I can make plans. I can be by your side or be your bodyguard. You do not, not for one second, need to do anything alone. We got you. You are so loved.

realizing they should leave but can't get out

Thank you for sharing that with me - and please know, everything you tell me is in the vault - your stories are secure with me. I love you and your safety and happiness is my priority. You are not alone. What's the first step we can take together here? What do you need? I can help you start making a plan that prioritizes your safety. I'm happy to Google and see what others have done in this situation. Just know that it seems really overwhelming and scary right now, but it won't always be. We'll navigate this together, as we've always done. Love you lots.

realizing they were/are in a relationship with a narcissist

You are holding so much, and so many emotions at once. I'm grateful you came to me and explained everything, and now you're not alone anymore. I want you to know how amazing, special, and loved you are. We will get through this together. I'm in awe of your strength. Right now things seem confusing, but soon enough, they won't. I'm here if you need me to save screenshots safely or feel free to text me things they said so you don't forget and they can't gaslight you later. It's going to be okay, we're going to weather this storm together. I love you, friend.

seemingly moving too fast with a new partner

I love hearing all of the details of this new and amazing time! They sound like a wonderful person, and I hope that they see how fantastic you are. Because you are. I know things are really exciting right now, and I just wanted to check in and make sure that you're taking a second to breathe, too. You are my priority, and I want you to know I'm here to listen to all of the thrilling deets, but also any concerns or hesitations, too. You're allowed to hold all of these feelings at once. I love you so much, and I'm just a text or FaceTime away.

still has to live with an ex post break up

Oh friend, right now everything is super a lot and overwhelming and all of the things. It's so hard when our space, our home, doesn't feel like ours, and we have to think about every little thing we're doing and saying. You are doing such a good job at being strong and brave, and I wish you didn't have to. I want to always remind you, you are not alone. Do you want me to research some new apartments? I can FaceTime you while you eat dinner in your room. We can meet up for a walk to get you some relief from the house. Right now seems really crappy, but it won't always be this way. I promise. You are wonderful and happier times are ahead.

texting an ex

Thank you for feeling safe enough to let me know what's going on, and I totally get it. It's hard! You two had so many life experiences together and it's so hard to let it all go at once. Do you need advice or just someone to listen? I'm here for whatever you need, you are my priority and I just don't want you to get hurt. You've worked so hard at healing from this, and I'm so proud of you. If you feel like you want to text them, you can text me instead! I'm always here, in your pocket. Whatever you do, know that I get it and I don't judge. I adore you and think you're the greatest!

thinking about reaching

out to an ex

Well, that is an idea. What are you looking to get from reaching out? I feel like if you're looking for closure or any satisfying interaction, you will most likely be disappointed. If you just can't fight the urge why don't you text me instead? I am here for you always.

scripts about the family

you're born to and

the family you create

what to say to your friend who is...

going no contact with family

or a loved one

First off, I am SO proud of you. I know this decision did not come lightly or quickly or without a lot of pain and consideration. Choosing yourself and protecting your wellbeing can be tough. Creating those boundaries is never easy, and is always something to be proud of. I'm holding you, and proud of you, and loving you always.

what to say to your friend who is…

supporting a loved one

through a loss

It can be so hard to watch someone you love navigate grief. Supporters need support and I'm here for you. I am going to text a few times a day to make sure you eat, drink water, and get some sleep. Send them my love and condolences and let me know if there is anything I can do to help.

planning a funeral for their parent

Well, making decisions during grief is one of the toughest moments in life. I'm here to help in any way I can. I can call caterers, florists, friends and family members. I know you're thinking about so many big things right now, so I'm bringing/sending dinner. Please make sure to keep drinking water and eat something, this is a shit time, but you need to take care of yourself too. I'm just so sorry for your loss and that you have to handle all of this. You are so strong, but I wish you didn't have to be. I love you so much.

taking care of a parent

You know, this is one of those times in life we don't believe will happen, and now you're here, and I'm just so proud of you for stepping up and being so brave. It's never easy to see someone you love go through hard shit, and you are so capable and strong. Please let me know if you need to vent at any time, I'm always in your pocket. I'll check in soon, never any need to reply, just know I'm here. Holding you close!

just found out a loved one passed

Oh my sweet friend, I am so sorry to hear this and for your loss. I'm here to talk or just to listen. I'd love to hear any stories you want to share about [Loved One's Name] and help you figure out any logistics that seem overwhelming. I'm going to bring/send you some coffee. I'm holding space for all of your feelings right now. You're never alone. We all love you so much.

cleaning out their parents' or guardians' house

I can only imagine how difficult and overwhelming this must be for you. This is a heavy task. Let me know if there is anything I can do or say that would help slightly reduce the weight for you. Take your time and take care of yourself. I love you. I am going to text you in three-ish hours to see how progress is. Send me pictures of anything funny/weird/sentimental you find!

what to say to your friend who...

has had the loss of a complicated family member

Ugh, it's always hard to lose someone we love, and loss can coincide with so many different emotions. You are allowed to hold more than one emotion at a time. You are strong, brave, and wonderful. Remember to take the time you need to process your feelings and grieve in your own way. I am always here for you and I love you.

dealing with declining parents

There is nothing easy about taking care of your parents or worrying about their wellbeing during these times. I'm always here to talk through options with you or simply to listen. I know you love them so much and watching them in this state is hard. There's no upside, it's just hard. I just want you to remember that you're supported, and loved, and so capable, and strong. I'm always just a text away.

dealing with their parents getting divorced as an adult

Oh my gosh, what an odd moment for you and your family. Divorce can be so complicated, and watching your parents go through these moments can be exhausting. Emotions will run high for a while and shit's going to be complicated and probably weird, but know that it will all eventually settle into a new normal and everyone will adjust. I am here if you need to vent. I love you!

what to say to your friend who is...

experiencing abuse in their home

My sweet friend, you are worthy of love, respect and security. Let's make a plan for what happens next together, you and your safety are my concern. I love you and am here for you. Let me know the safest way to contact you, and know that I am here 24/7. We got this. You are not alone.

has a loved one experiencing a relapse

How difficult to see a loved one going through such a hard time. It's so scary that relapsing is a part of the recovery process. I imagine you're feeling really helpless right now, so know that I'm holding you close. I love you and I'm here to listen to any worries anytime. I'll check in soon and send you some Muppet GIFs.

going through a friend break up

Why does nobody talk about how difficult friend breakups are?! This shit is tough, and I'm so proud of you for surviving something so heartbreaking. You are such a fantastic friend and I'm so grateful you're in my life. I love you and I'm here to listen anytime. Remember, I'm just a text away!

what to say to your friend who…

just found out a friend passed

My love, I am so sorry. This is heartbreaking and I'm holding you close. This just sucks and there's no other way about it. I'd love to hear about your wonderful friend, if you'd be in the place to tell me about them. Sending you so much love. I'm here if you need anything. I'll check in later.

just found out their parents aren't their biological parents

Wow, that's a lot of big news. I would imagine this is difficult and confusing, and remember even though everything feels weird and shaken up, that so many people love and support you. Remember, family is not just about biology, it's about the love and connection you have with the people around you. I'm here to listen, and always just a text away. Life is an odd adventure, but I'm always by your side.

just found their biological parents

WELL, what a journey! How are you feeling about this? I'm holding so much space for all the excited, sad and complicated emotions. However you decide to proceed, I'm always on your side, and I'm here with you and would love nothing more than to chat through your thoughts. What a whirlwind! Proud of you for pursuing the tough questions!

what to say to your friend who...

just found their biological siblings

Siblings! Exciting stuff. Good for you for pursuing this big scary life changing thing. Whatever you decide to do next, I'm here to love and support you! Let me know if you want to chat about your plan moving forward. I love you so much and I'm here to vent/chat/listen. I think we can both agree that this shit is WILD!

has a complicated relationship with their parent or guardian who is in bad health

Thank you for sharing this with me. I'm sure you must be feeling a lot of complicated things right now, and that's okay. I'm validating that this is a lot! Remember that you are not alone and I'm here for you. Watching a parent go through this can be so emotional, and on top of that, adding in your relationship with them probably stirs up a lot of feelings. I'm sending you so much love and empathy right now. Let's navigate this together and find the support you need. You are strong and capable and I'll be here to support you no matter what.

has a parent or guardian
in bad health

Oh my love, I'm so sorry you all are going through this. I know how close you two are and what an important light they are to you. Please send them my love and know that I'm here to support you both however I can. I want to give you lots of space to spend quality time together, so I'm not going to call or text much, but know I am here the second you need me! Love you lots and I'm holding you close in my heart.

what to say to your friend who is...

still dealing with warring parents years after their divorce

Sheesh, I know it's been tough dealing with your parents' ongoing issues, you'd think they'd be chill by now. You are so strong and resilient, but I wish you didn't have to be. You deserve to have peace and happiness in your life, and I'll always be here to support you. Remember, you are not alone and you are loved. I am here to chat and listen if you need to vent. And don't forget to text me whenever they say something bizarre! Parents, man. They don't make it easy.

what to say to your friend who is…

trying to find a care facility for their relative

Ugh, dealing with this stuff is hard and sad and so painfully slow and expensive! I am here for you to discuss options with. I am also here if you need to vent. Just know whatever choice you make is the right choice. Please let me know if you are feeling overwhelmed and if it all feels like too much pressure. Whatever it feels like, I've got you. Call me anytime and we can discuss anything you need to talk about. Love you, buddy.

anxious about introducing the new baby to their pet

Big life moments can be overwhelming and this is one of them! I know you're a little nervous about introducing the babe to [pet], so just remember that this is a transition time and if it seems overwhelming or hard right now, it won't always be. I promise! You're an amazing [dog/cat/llama] parent, and soon enough the two of them will be in kahootz. You got this!! Send me photos!

has had a pet pass away

Oh love, I am so sorry. My heart completely breaks for you. There is nothing anyone can do or say to make this better. But know you were the best pet parent and they had such a great life by your side. [Pet name] will always be in your heart and I would love to hear stories about them if you want to share. I will keep checking in on you.

has a pet going into surgery

You and I both know that you are an exceptional pet parent and that there is no one more capable of making choices for you sweet [Pet Name]. They are in good hands with the crew at your vet's office. What time do they go in? I will be texting you GIFs to make you laugh and be there with you while you're in the waiting room. [Pet Name] is in my heart and my thoughts. Please keep me updated on their progress, if that's comfortable for you.

having anxiety about a new pet

So many feelings! Having a new pet is a lot – and I want to validate that for you! Just take a breath and know that these feelings won't last forever. Take it one step at a time, one day at a time, and soon enough, a new normal will appear. I can't wait to see pics of the new [pet], and soon enough things will feel less overwhelming!

scripts about kids

just announced they are pregnant

That is such great news! Thank you so much for sharing that with me. How are you feeling? I am so excited to get to celebrate this new life and share this time with you. I can't wait to meet this little human! Keep me updated on babe's progress. So excited for you!

is or was up all night

with a sick kid

Oh man, sounds like a rough night. I'm so sorry! Take a breath and remember this won't last forever, even though it feels like it will, I promise it won't. Is there anything you need or I can send over for you? I'm validating how hard it is to have sick kiddos at home, and you're allowed to be annoyed and frustrated! It sucks! Here to send funny memes, just let me know. Love you!

what to say to your friend who is...

suffering pregnancy loss

My sweet friend, I'm just so sorry. This sucks and there's no other way about it. Please remember to just keep breathing. One breath at a time. Put on some soft, comfy clothes, cuddle up in bed, and let yourself feel the feelings. I'm here if you need anything day or night. I'll check in later, no need to reply, just know I'm right here. I love you, babe.

experiencing sleep deprivation

There is nothing worse than living life in a zombie state – and truly, there is nothing more exhausting than the sleep deprivation that comes after a night with a screaming baby. Sending you a huge hug and know that I see how hard you're working and how tired you are. This won't last forever, I promise. You got this. I'm right here if you need me.

missing their kids when they're with the other parent

I know you're missing the kiddles a lot right now, and I'm validating for you how strange it must be to not have them with you! I bet it's a weird sensation and I know you're worried about them. Do you want to FaceTime or watch a movie and text together? Remember, as much as you miss them, I'm also giving you permission to enjoy your quiet time and have a dance party. They'll be back soon enough, and next time, this won't sting quite as much. I love you, you amazing human!

has anxiety about introducing their first born to their new baby

I totally know that it can be nerve wracking thinking about introducing the new babe to the kids, it's a lot of emotions! And, even the exciting emotions can be overwhelming sometimes. Remember that you're not alone in this, and we're all here for you all. It's so, so normal to have some anxiety about how the older kids will react and adjust to a new baby in the house. It's an adjustment for everyone. Let's navigate this together and find the support you need. You are strong and capable, and a seriously amazing parent. I love you!

has anxiety about leaving their first child to give birth to a new baby

I know you're feeling a little anxious about leaving [First Child] to have the baby. It's a big life moment, and I want you to remember that you're not alone, and you are SO strong and brave. It's incredibly normal to have mixed feelings and anxiety about going to have a new baby while your first baby is at home! Just remember that this moment in time will pass and become a wonderful memory for the baby book soon. I love you, friend!

what to say to your friend who...

has anxiety about deciding to have another child

The decision to have another child is overwhelming and sometimes it feels like there's no right answer, and you know what? There isn't. But, here's what I do know: you're an amazing parent and any child would be lucky to be in your family. Let me know if you want to word vomit your worries out to me, no shame, no judgment, just get it out. I'm always here to listen. Whatever you decide, we love you and support you.

has anxiety around breastfeeding

Oh babe, breastfeeding can be so difficult, you are so, so not alone. It's totally normal to be overwhelmed, touched out, confused, all the things!! Just please remember this: whatever you decide to do for you and the baby is the right decision. Most importantly, remember that you are loved, supported, and an amazing mother. You are doing a fantastic job, and we are all so proud of you.

what to say to your friend who…

has anxiety deciding whether or not to have a medicated birth

I know you've been struggling with the decision about having a medicated birth, and I just want you to know that I see you and how much thought you're putting into the plans. Let me know if you want to talk it all out, I'm more than happy to listen, no-judgment, just an ear. I do know that whatever decision you end up making will be the right one for you and the baby, and I'm so proud of you. I can't wait to snuggle the babe!

becoming a stepparent

Becoming a stepparent is a huge life moment, and I hear it can be an exciting, emotional, and challenging journey. You are an amazing, loving, and kind human and [Stepchild] is lucky to have you in their life. I'm always here to listen when you need to vent during this life transition. [Stepchild] is a fantastic kiddo and I'm so excited to hear all about your adventures together. You're going to kill it at this step-parenting gig and I'm so proud of you.

has a child going through a health scare and is waiting for test results

Oh my gosh, waiting is truly the worst. I want you to know I'm holding so much space for your worry, concern and anxiety. I'm here to support you all however I can. I can just hang on the phone with you or give you space or send silly GIFs. Either way, I'm going to check in to make sure you know I'm here, but feel free not to answer if that's too much right now. Love you all so much.

what to say to your friend who is…

co-parenting with a difficult

co-parent

You've been through a lot lately, and the last thing you need is to co-parent with a very difficult person, and I just wanted to tell you that I'm so proud of you and how you're handling the situation. You are an amazing parent and I know you're working incredibly hard to hold it all together. Remember, you are not alone, I'm always here for you, to listen and support you through these stressful moments.

what to say to your friend who...

has suffered infant or

newborn loss

Oh my sweet friend, I am holding you close in my arms and heart. Please do not hesitate to reach out if you need anything. I am sending you all so much love. I will be thinking of you all and sending so many prayers your way. What is their name? I'd be honored to hear all about your baby when you're ready. I am keeping you all close in my heart and will check in soon. I love you all.

has decided to terminate

a pregnancy

I'm so proud of you for navigating an overwhelming decision, and it's a choice that I know you gave a lot of thought to. I honor you for choosing what is best for you. Let me know if I can help you figure out any logistics. I'd be happy to drive you/arrange your transportation and make sure you have a clean, cozy place to recoup and some comfort food after. I'm going to look into what you'll need in the immediate aftermath and make sure you have it all as best I can. If you want to talk, I'm here to hold you through any of the feelings you have around the decision. Otherwise, I will just keep checking in on you, feel free to not respond, but know I am always holding you in my heart.

what to say to your friend who is…

deciding to keep baby

Wow, that is some exciting news! I am so proud of you for making such big life decisions, and I see the care and consideration you put into making this decision. You are so brave for leading with your heart and listening to your intuition. Let me know if there is anything you need. I'm so excited to welcome this little baby into the world and watch you become an amazing parent. I love you lots.

suffered an early term
miscarriage

Oh friend, thank you for sharing this with me. I'm holding you close. Is there anything you need? Do you want me to stay on the phone with you? I can keep FaceTime on as you rest so you're not alone. This is shitty and please know you're allowed to feel however you feel right now. I love you so much, babe.

what to say to your friend who is...

making the decision to freeze their eggs

I know that this is a big decision, and of course it's totally normal to feel nervous about the journey. Remember that you are never alone during this process, and I'm here for you. I'm just a text away! You are strong and capable and I'm so proud of you. I love you and I support you in whatever you choose.

undergoing an embryo transfer

Big day, my friend! I would imagine that going through this transfer today is both totally exciting and utterly nerve-wracking. Remember that you are not alone, I'm always here for you. Take a deep breath, shake your shoulders out, and let's hope for the best. I am so excited that at the end of this there will be a new little baby to love, and I can't wait to watch you flourish as a parent!

adopting a child or baby

Friend, this is so exciting! I'm thrilled to hear this news – you are an amazing human, and will be a fantastic, loving, and compassionate parent. I cannot wait to hear more details and meet this wonderful little baby/child. Keep me updated on any and all news and know that I am right here if you need anything.

experiencing a failed IVF round

Well, this sucks, and I'm so sorry. I'm here if you need anything. I'm going to send you some treats and let's FaceTime and watch a movie this week. You are a fucking badass and I'm so proud of you for making brave decisions. I love you so much, and I'm here literally day or night if you need to vent, cry, scream, or just sit silently on the phone together. Sending you so many hugs.

experiencing their child
being bullied

Fuck man, kids are the worst. I'm so sorry that this is going on with [Kid]. You are an amazing parent, and [Kid] is one of my favorite little humans, and I'm livid that this is happening. Let me know if you need help writing an email or text. I've got you both. I know it doesn't seem like it now, but things will be okay soon.

feeling weird about taking on the role of mother

Becoming a mom can be a real mind-fuck, and I need you to know that your feelings are valid and real. I'm so proud of the way you're handling this huge life change and please remember that you are not alone, we're all here to support you in whatever you need. Taking on a new role in life can be really overwhelming, and you don't need to embrace it all at once, it can be a gradual process, and you will get there. You are capable, strong, and beautiful inside and out, and I'm so grateful you're in my life.

feels bad about not loving every minute of parenthood

Yeah, I know parenthood is a LOT. You're def not alone! This shit is hard! You're doing great and I'm so proud of you. You're killing it and your kids are so lucky to have you. Never forget that you are a truly fantastic parent and human, and I'm so grateful you're my friend!

experiencing disappointment upon finding out baby's sex

I know you're feeling a lot of confusing things about learning the sex of the baby. Remember, your feelings are valid, and I hope that you know that your feelings are not representative of your excitement to be a parent, or your love for the baby. Sometimes things don't happen in the way we think they will, and that doesn't make them bad or wrong, we just have to feel the feelings. Let me know if you need someone to just listen. Remember that you are not alone, and we're all here for you.

going back to the workplace after having a baby

I know that you're feeling all the things about going back to work right now. Just remember, all of your feelings are totally valid! Balancing parenthood and work can be overwhelming to think about, but I want you to know you are a badass human, parent, and friend, and I am so proud of you. [Baby] will be totally fine, you'll do your thing, and then you can come home and change back into sweats. You're killing it at this adulting gig.

going through a custody battle

You're already going through so much, and this added stress about custody is just a LOT – and I am validating that. I see how hard you're working to hold it all together, and I want you to know you're an aggressively amazing parent and your kids are so lucky to have you. It seems really, really hard right now, but I promise there is a light at the end of the tunnel. I'm here anytime you need to vent or cry. I can FaceTime the kids and tell them stupid jokes so you can go cry in the bathroom or call your lawyer. I love you, friend.

having trouble breastfeeding

First of all, you are an amazing parent, and you made a small human. That is a huge accomplishment, love! Breastfeeding can be confusing and painful and tough, but you are doing a kickass job and you should be so proud of yourself. Remember, you and [Baby] are still learning the whole process, and it can take time. You are not alone, I'm here for you. Would it be okay if I sent some resources your way? You've got this.

having trouble conceiving

Thank you for sharing this with me. I know that it can be super overwhelming to even admit that it is not shaping up to be the experience you anticipated. I'm here if you need help researching doctors or anything you need. I'm so proud of you for being brave and investigating what's going on. The disconnect from your body can feel so real, I am here to vent if you need! You are a badass for navigating everything right now.

has an Independent Educational Program meeting coming up for their kid

I know today may seem overwhelming, but I want you to remember that you are a bad-ass, amazing parent and you know [your kid] better than anyone. I'm so proud of you, and just remember to breathe, bring a bottle of water, and get yourself a treat afterwards. Do you need help drafting any scripts or notes beforehand? I'm here if you need anything. Let me know how it goes. You got this.

has their in laws coming to town to visit their newborn

Oh lord, could anyone make your life easy? LOL. Just hide in your room and let them change those diapers! Text me any weird shit your MIL says. I love you, you got this!

what to say to your friend who is...

on an IVF journey

First of all, I want you to know I am proud of you, this shit is hard and complicated. I am here for all the details, to vent about insurance and to hear how the shots go. This is the beginning of a very exciting life moment, and I'm here to remind you of that when it gets tough and frustrating. I just love you so much and I'm excited to support you through this new journey. I know the hormones might make you feel off, so I'll keep checking in and you share as much as you want. I love you and I'm here to support you through it all!

just got their period when they're trying to get pregnant

Ugh, that just sucks, and I'm so sorry. There's really nothing else to say except, that sucks. I see how disappointed you are and I'm so proud of you for being so freaking brave and amazing for going through this journey. Check your email for a Starbucks card later, and get yourself something really sugary, with lots of whipped cream. I love you so much, and I'm always here.

has a child in the hospital

Hey, thanks for letting me know about [Kid]. Is there anything I can do? I know you're overwhelmed, so no need to reply right now, but know that I'm on the other end of the line and I can Google anything you need day or night. When the doctor comes in feel free to call me so I can be your second set of ears. Send me technical terms to look up for you. Sending you all so much love and thinking of you all. Keep me posted when you can.

planning a funeral for their child

I am holding you close and I am here for whatever you need. I can call people, I can make arrangements, I can help with laundry or sending food. I can sit with the kids so you can cry in the car. This is a nightmare, but you are not alone. I'll keep checking in, no need to respond, but please know I am here for literally anything, day or night. I love you all.

experiencing postpartum depression

Thank you for sharing all of that with me. I am validating that postpartum is a really fucking hard time, and you most likely don't feel like yourself, let alone a human being. Remember that you're not alone! I'm right here. Always. Do you need help asking for something? Do you need me to send anything? Let's navigate this together and find the support you need. It's not a sign of weakness to ask for help and it's important to take care of yourself. You are strong and capable and you will get through this.

has gotten concerning results on tests for their pregnancy, is waiting on more information

Waiting is the worst, and I'm so sorry you're in this limbo right now. It's the actual worst. Please know I'm holding space for you and here if you need anyone to do a quick Google search or just send a meme. Call me whenever you want, I'll check in soon to see if there are any updates. Love you lots.

experiencing pregnancy issues

Ugh, I know this is all so much to handle and so confusing. Not having answers can be so overwhelming and frustrating. Please know I see how hard you're working to figure shit out and navigate this process. I'm here if you need to vent about anything or need a little help Googling. I love you, friend.

reeling after being shamed for publicly breastfeeding

What is wrong with people? I am so fucking sorry. You're a kick-ass parent who is literally giving life nourishment to your gorgeous babe and people are so creepy and backwards. I totally understand being pissed about this, but this is on them, not you! You're an inspiration, my friend!

has sadness around
birthing experience

Thank you for sharing those feelings with me. Sometimes when things don't go as we expected, it can really throw us for a loop and it can become totally dysregulating. Just know that you did the best you could with the situation, and we are all so proud of you. Would it help to journal some of these feelings out? I'm holding space if you want to release any of the feelings. I want to validate that your feelings are legit and heard. I'm so sorry the experience didn't go as planned. Here for you.

selling their children's home

Moving is always incredibly stressful, and I know you're feeling so many varied emotions around this big life change. I just want you to know that I see how hard you're working to create a beautiful life for your family, and a house is just a home because of the people in it. You are an amazing parent and whatever you decide to do will be in the best interest of everyone. I can't wait to buy you a new set of dish towels in [their favorite pattern/color] from your registry, you deserve this fresh start and I'm so proud of you!

trying to get their baby
on a sleep schedule

Just sending a quick text to say you got this! Baby sleep stuff is THE WORST, and you're def not alone. Just hang in there and remember it's a long game, and you're doing your best. You're an amazing parent and we're all cheering you on. One sleep at a time, friend! I'll be up if you need funny memes sent your way!

postpartum and having a tough time with family members

Oh friend, you're holding so much right now. I just wanted you to know that I see you and I hear you, and I know you are doing your very best. Please remember that everyone has their own baggage and agenda, and I am giving you permission to completely ignore people who may make you feel crappy. How can I best support you right now? Please know you are not alone and I'm right here if you need anything. I'm validating that this is a rough time, and it won't always be, but if it feels heavy right now, it's because it is. You are a wonderful human and a fantastic parent and I'm so proud of you.

just found out they're having surprise multiples

Well, that's some news! How are we feeling about this? You're going to be an amazing parent to these babies and I'm so excited to be on this journey with you. Text me when you can and let me know how it all went down when you found out. And, if you're feeling a lot of feelings right now, just remember, it's okay to feel many things at once! Always here if you need anything.

experiencing an unplanned pregnancy with their partner

Oh, big news! Thank you for sharing this with me. How are we feeling about everything? Lots of feelings all at once? I'm here to listen to them all and talk it through with you, if that's what you'd like. I'm here for bouncing ideas, worries and excitements. It's all valid! Just remember that whatever choices you make, I am here, and I love and support you all.

just unexpectedly found out they're pregnant and is thrilled about it

What! How exciting! I cannot wait to love on that little person. I know this wasn't exactly as you planned, but I am so thrilled for you! You are going to be a fantastic parent, and I am thrilled to see you flourish in the role! Mazel, baby!

experiencing an unplanned pregnancy with a stranger

Oh love, thank you for sharing this with me. First of all, take a breath. You're not alone. Do you want to talk about how you're feeling? Sometimes getting the words out about this stuff helps you figure out some feelings. I'm here to help you plan out how to let them know the info and talk about whatever you decide to do. I've got you, and we've got this. Let's grab some snacks and plan this out together on FaceTime. You are surrounded by people that love you, and we will figure it all out!

what to say to your friend who…

has been told they need to terminate a pregnancy due to health issues

Oh my love, I am so sorry. I'm holding you close and know that you're not alone. I'll be thinking of you all and I'm here if you need literally anything. I love you.

waiting to see if they're miscarrying or have miscarried

Oh friend, I'm holding you close during this limbo. I know things seem really awful and scary right now, but I want you to know you're not alone. I'm here, we're here, and we're going to be by your side no matter what. You are so loved. I'll be here if you need anything.

dropping their kid or kids off at daycare for first time

Big day! Just wanted to send you a boost of love, as I know you were feeling so many big feelings about this day! Remember to take a breath and that this is a transition time, so if things seem overwhelming or emotional today, tomorrow is a new day. [Kid] is going to be just fine, and so will you. You are an amaaaaazing parent, and I'm so proud of you. Please keep me updated on everyone!

has a child in lockdown at school

Thank you for letting me know what's going on – this is incredibly scary, and I'm validating that for you. Please keep me posted, and let me know if you need me to Google anything or call anyone. I'm holding you close and I'm just a text away. Thinking of your sweet babies and you. Love you.

scripts about jobs and careers

getting due recognition
for their work

HELL YES! Glad they're recognizing my amazing friend! You deserve it. Enjoy the applause and make sure to document it for future reviews/job applications. So proud of you, but not at all surprised. You're amazing!

what to say to your friend who...

isn't sure if they should

take a new job

First off, I'm proud of you for taking a beat to consider your options. Obviously, I support your decision whatever it may be. Remember that you deserve to be in a job that brings you fulfillment and happiness. Trust your gut, you know what's best for you. Why don't you take two days and commit to the idea of taking the job to see how that feels? We can do a gut check after. Always here to make a pros/cons list and just be an ear to listen. We've got this.

was recently laid off

Oh my sweet friend, I am here for you, and I understand how difficult this must be for you. Remember that you are not alone. I and so many others love you and know what a big blow this feels like. You are strong and resilient and I believe in you. Let me know how I can help! Do you want me to send you jobs in a few days? Or just cute puppy pics? I'm here day or night, just a text away. I know it feels like a lot right now, so I'll check in soon to see how you're doing.

what to say to your friend who is...

starting a company

I am so proud of you for taking this step and following your dreams. You are so amazingly capable and talented, and I believe in your success. I can't wait to see your company grow and flourish. Let me know how I can support you and the new company! Just so incredibly proud of you!

just got rejected from a
job they wanted

Oof. I am so sorry! What a disappointment. Remember that rejection is a part of life, and it does not define your worth. Keep pushing forward, a better opportunity is waiting for you. I love you and I'm here if you need to vent!

what to say to your friend who is...

fundraising for their company

Wow, what a big and exciting step! I'm so proud of you for making this brave business decision. Remember, you're not alone and I'm always here to listen and remind you how badass you are. You're strong and resilient and I believe in you. Please let me know how I can help and if there's anything I can do to pull in your community to support you too!

what to say to your friend who is...

going back to the workplace after an absence

Hi friend, I know tomorrow is a big day. How are we feeling about it? Nervous? Excited? Both? It all tracks! Make a great lunch plan and text me to let me know how it goes. It may feel like you've forgotten what you do during these last few months, but I'm sure you'll be back in the swing of things in no time. You are amazing and everyone must all be so pumped to have you back. I'm just a text away, keep me posted!

just got a new job offer

YAAAS! Of course they offered you the job! You are amazing! How are you feeling about the offer? I am here to talk through everything. I am so proud of you. Finding a new job is so stressful and you nailed it!

what to say to your friend who is…

starting a new career

I am so excited for you and your new journey! You're so brave and I am so proud of you for choosing yourself and your future. I can't wait to see you thrive on this new career path. I'm always here to remind you how kick-ass you are!

what to say to your friend who is...

starting a new job

I am so proud of you, and I'm so excited for this new chapter in your life. Remember that you are capable and talented, and I believe in your amazing success. I can't wait to hear about the first day, text me during lunch if you can!

About the Authors

Olivia Dreizen Howell and Genevieve "Jenny" Dreizen are the co-founders of Fresh Starts Registry, the first and only platform for everything you need to begin again. Founded in 2021, Fresh Starts Registry is your one-stop-shop for all of the support items and experts you need to empower you through brave, bold, and big life decisions. Olivia Dreizen Howell is a marketing expert, mom of two boys, and currently lives on Long Island. Genevieve Dreizen is a design and operations obsessive, joy enthusiast and future expat. Together the sisters are excited to collaborate on books, continue expanding Fresh Starts Registry and support their people.

www.ingramcontent.com/pod-product-compliance
Lightning Source LLC
Chambersburg PA
CBHW060251150626
46553CB00019BA/1751